On the Move

BUSES

Ursula Pang

PowerKiDS press

PK Beginners

Look at all the buses!

212
SCHOOL BUS
214
215
SCHOOL BUS

School buses take kids to school.

WATCH

Buses are full of seats.

SEAT

Be safe on the bus!
Stay in your seat.

Every bus has a driver.

SCHOOL BUS
BUS DRIVER

The bus lights flash!
The driver stops to let
someone on the bus.

LIGHTS
SCHOOL BUS
EMERGENCY DOOR
STOP
BUS STOP
LIGHTS
SCHOOL

Cities have
many buses.

Some people take
a bus to work.

Some buses have two floors!

3

Some people take long bus trips.

Would you like to take a bus trip?

Published in 2025 by The Rosen Publishing Group, Inc.
2544 Clinton Street, Buffalo, NY 14224

First Edition

Editor: Greg Roza
Book Design: Rachel Rising

Photo Credits: Cover, p. 1 Mikbiz/Shutterstock.com; p. 3 pyzata/Shutterstock.com; p. 5 4 PM production/Shutterstock.com; p. 7 Pat Shrader/Shutterstock.com; p. 9 Pressmaster/Shutterstock.com; p. 11 Prostock-studio/Shutterstock.com; p. 13 rSnapshotPhotos/Shutterstock.com; p. 15 kolt_duo/Shutterstock.com; p. 17 Zamrznuti tonovi/Shutterstock.com; p. 19 Sergii Figurnyi/Shutterstock.com; p. 21 Hanhalo Yehor/Shutterstock.com; p. 23 Drazen Zigic/Shutterstock.com.

Library of Congress Cataloging-in-Publication Data

Names: Pang, Ursula, author.
Title: Buses / Ursula Pang.
Description: Buffalo : PowerKids Press, (2025) | Series: On the move
Identifiers: LCCN 2023050565 (print) | LCCN 2023050566 (ebook) | ISBN 9781499444605 (library binding) | ISBN 9781499444599 (paperback) | ISBN 9781499444612 (ebook)
Subjects: LCSH: Buses--Juvenile literature.
Classification: LCC TL232 .P26 2025 (print) | LCC TL232 (ebook) | DDC 629.222/33--dc23/eng/20231107
LC record available at https://lccn.loc.gov/2023050565
LC ebook record available at https://lccn.loc.gov/2023050566

Manufactured in the United States of America